Bradbury, Ray, 1920-
The haunted computer and the android pope / Ray Bradbury. -- New York : Knopf, 1981.
98 p. ; 22 cm.

ISBN 0-394-51444-0 : $8.95

I. Title.

ALSO BY RAY BRADBURY

THE STORIES OF RAY BRADBURY

WHERE ROBOT MICE AND ROBOT MEN RUN ROUND IN ROBOT TOWNS

LONG AFTER MIDNIGHT

WHEN ELEPHANTS LAST IN THE DOORYARD BLOOMED

THE HALLOWEEN TREE

I SING THE BODY ELECTRIC!

THE MACHINERIES OF JOY

THE ANTHEM SPRINTERS

SOMETHING WICKED THIS WAY COMES

A MEDICINE FOR MELANCHOLY

DANDELION WINE

SWITCH ON THE NIGHT

THE OCTOBER COUNTRY

MOBY DICK (screenplay)

FAHRENHEIT 451

THE GOLDEN APPLES OF THE SUN

THE ILLUSTRATED MAN

THE MARTIAN CHRONICLES

DARK CARNIVAL

THE HAUNTED COMPUTER
AND THE ANDROID POPE

RAY BRADBURY

THE HAUNTED COMPUTER AND THE ANDROID POPE

ALFRED · A · KNOPF · NEW YORK · 1981

THIS IS A BORZOI BOOK

PUBLISHED BY ALFRED A. KNOPF, INC.

Published in the United States
by Alfred A. Knopf, Inc., New York,
and simultaneously in Canada
by Random House of Canada Limited, Toronto.
Distributed by Random House, Inc., New York.
Some of the poems in this book have been previously
published by Future Life, Lord John Press,
The Los Angeles Times, The San Diego Union,
Santa Susana Press, Science Digest, Questar,
and Westways.
Library of Congress Cataloging in Publication Data
Bradbury, Ray, [date]
The haunted computer and the android pope.
I. Title.
PS3503.R167H38 1981 811'.54 80-2724
ISBN 0-394-51444-0
Manufactured in the United States of America
First Edition

With love for my granddaughter, Julia, whose
face promises me immortality

THE HAUNTED COMPUTER
AND THE ANDROID POPE

THE HAUNTED COMPUTER AND THE ANDROID POPE

Haunted Computer, Android Pope,
One serves data, the other hope.
The late-night ghosts of man's dire needs
Are snacks on which computer feeds
To harvest zeros, sum the sums,
Knock something wicked ere it comes,
And drop dumb evil to its knees
With inked electric snickersnees.
While Android Pope takes up from there,
Where physics stops mid-flight, mid-air,
There Papa's primed electric mind
Grows faith in countries of the blind.
Where mass and gravity bulk huge—
Andromeda its centrifuge—
Or matter dwindles to mere flea,
There Android Pope makes papal tea
To serve to doubtful Thomas me
And thee and thine and thine and thee;
Last suppers his to circuit there
Where physics loses self in air,
And man surprised by large or small
Sees naught beyond the two at all.
That is the moment where, well-met,
Electric Pope/Computer fret
Where stuff gives up its ways and means
And emptiness fills in-betweens

Where label-less the mystery goes
In veils and prides of cosmic snows
Which rationed out by God beyond
Are light-year sea and lake and pond
Which shallow are but drowned in deeps'
Computer mind that finds and keeps
But cannot answer final thirst:
Which, egg or chicken, arrived first?
The primal motive hides in stars
Where astronauts in rocket cars
Will never solve it, so bright Pope
With fireworks inside for hope,
With tapes for tripes, A.C.–D.C.
Speaks metaphors from Galilee
And bakes good bread and serves a wine
That bloods the soul most super-fine
And emptiness fills up with words
Like flocking flights of firebirds
That move and motion, merge and mull
So men gone empty now are full.
Yet, all mysterious remains,
So man stands out in ghosting rains
And makes umbrellas with machines
Half-satisfied with in-betweens,
His life twin mysteries given hope
By Ghost Computer, Android Pope.

GO NOT WITH RUINS IN YOUR MIND

Go not with ruins in your mind
Or beauty fails; Rome's sun is blind
And catacomb your cold hotel
Where should-be heaven's could-be hell.
Beware the temblors and the flood
That time hides fast in tourist's blood
And shambles forth from hidden home
At sight of lost-in-ruins Rome.
Think on your joyless blood, take care,
Rome's scattered bricks and bones lie there
In every chromosome and gene
Lie all that was, or might have been.
All architectural tombs and thrones
Are tossed to ruin in your bones.
Time earthquakes there all life that grows
And all your future darkness knows,
Take not these inner ruins to Rome,
A sad man wisely stays at home;
For if your melancholy goes
Where all is lost, then your loss grows
And all the dark that self employs
Will teem—so travel then with joys.
Or else in ruins consummate
A death that waited long and late,
And all the burning towns of blood
Will shake and fall from sane and good,

And you with ruined sight will see
A lost and ruined Rome. And thee?
Cracked statue mended by noon's light
Yet innerscaped with soul's midnight.
So go not traveling with mood
Or lack of sunlight in your blood,
Such traveling has double cost,
When you and empire *both* are lost.
When your mind storm-drains catacomb,
And all seems graveyard rock in Rome—
Tourist, go not.
Stay home.
Stay home!

I've seen a thousand homes go down the tracks
Away, away . . .
Late night or early morn,
There goes the house, all white, where I was born.
My traveling train
Gives back to me by moon or noontime's rain
The house, the house, the house
Where I'm reborn again.
As common as sparrows in flight,
There flies by my front porch and me,
Out of sight, out of sight.
We are common together: common house,
    common weather,
Common boy on a bike on a cool dark night lawn,
Sinking in clover,
Or boy on brick street at dawn, roofing a ball:
Annie over! Annie over!
Where I'll pop up next, Peoria or Paducah, I don't know;
All I can say is:
Here I come, here I come,
There I go, there I go!
Always the same boy, bright-eyed as a mouse,
Always the same folks on the porch of that house,
Swinging by in the light,
Drowning deep in the night,

There they drift, there they fly
At the train whistle's cry:
O good-bye, O good-bye.
Lawn and porch on the run; boy's face like the sun
Looking up through the rain
As again and again, the boy who was me
Climbs a branch, drops from tree,
But arrives to depart
While his shout cracks my heart.
Lord, does anyone see
All those boys who are me,
And does anyone know all those homes white as snow
That like riverboats glide
In the tide of the train as it takes me away?
Who can say, who can say?
Just my time machine moves
Through the land of my loves,
And more houses and boys and more trees and more lawns
Wait there just ahead in the circling dawns.
A procession of dreams!
O, isn't God clever?
He's cloned me in teams.
So? I'll live here forever!

NOR IS THE AIM OF MAN TO STAY BENEATH A STONE

They say that we must falter, fail, and fall away
To all that's lost;
I say the cost is overmuch
I'd spend us better with our will.
The mills of our machine-made gods grind swift *not* slow,
I with their lightning-arcs and wild illuminations go
To light a path
Not to the grave but walking on the air
On stairs of weather, cloud, and sky.
I would not doom us with those easy repetitions
Of old kettledrumming dooms
I heard from childhood on in dull, drab,
Ideas long since gone to incestuous
Intellectuals' rooms . . .
Where they make litanies of night to scare their souls
And turn from birds and skies and stars
To imitate death moles or morbid beetles ticking death
Which if we let them would dig deep in time and keep
Our flesh in most inconsequent black holes.
That's not my game,
Nor is the aim of man to stay beneath a stone.
To own the universe, our aim. And *never* die.
That's mine, and yours, and yours, and yours,
To shame dumb death, leave Earth to dust, tread moon,
Vault Mars, and win the stars with flame . . .
Or know the reason why.

JOY IS THE GRACE WE SAY TO GOD

Joy is the grace we say to God
For His gifts given.
It is the leavening of time,
It splits our bones with lightning,
Fills our marrow
With a harrowing of light
And seeds our blood with sun,
And thus we
Put out the night
And then
Put out the night.
Tears make an end of things;
So weep, yes, weep.
But joy says, after that, not done . . .
No, not by any means. Not done!
Take breath and shout it out!
That laugh, that cry which says: Begin again,
So all's reborn, begun!
Now hear this, Eden's child,
Remember in thy green Earth heaven,
All beauty-shod:
Joy is the grace we say to God.

They have not seen the stars,
Not one, not one
Of all the creatures on this world
In all the ages since the sands first touched the wind
Not one, not one,
No beast of all the beasts has stood
On meadowland or plain or hill
And known the thrill of looking at those fires;
Our soul admires what they, oh, they, have never known.
Five billion years have flown in turnings of the spheres
But not once in all those years
Has lion, dog, or bird that sweeps the air
Looked there, oh, look. Looked there, ah God, the stars;
Oh, look, look there!
It is as if all time had never been,
Or universe or sun or moon or simple morning light.
Their tragedy was mute and blind, and so remains.
Our sight?
Yes, *ours*? To know now what we are.
But think of it, then choose—now, which?
Born to raw Earth, inhabiting a scene
And all of it, no sooner viewed, erased, gone blind
As if these miracles had never been.
Vast circlings of sounding light, of fire and frost,
And all so quickly seen then quickly lost?
Or us, in fragile flesh, with God's new eyes

That lift and comprehend and search the skies?
We watch the seasons drifting in the lunar tide
And know the years, remembering what's died.

Oh, yes, perhaps some birds some nights
Have felt Orion rise and tuned their flights
And turned southward
Because star-charts were printed in their sweet
    genetic dreams—
Or so it seems.
But, *see*? But *really* see and *know*?
And, knowing, want to touch those fires,
To grow until the mighty brow of man Lamarckian-tall
Knocks earthquakes, striking moon,
Then Mars, then Saturn's rings;
And, growing, hope to show
All other beasts just how
To fly with dreams instead of ancient wings.
So, think on this: we're first! the only ones
Whom God has honored with his rise of suns.
For us as gifts Aldebaran, Centauri, homestead Mars.
Wake up, God says. Look there. Go fetch.
The stars. Oh, Lord, much thanks. The stars!

THIS ATTIC WHERE THE MEADOW GREENS

This attic where the meadow greens
Now keeps itself a world between two worlds,
One world of weather, one of blood and dream.
Its architectural scheme there high above
Was to make heaps and sprawls of silent time
Abide it there to know a slower beat
Than any river street or dogprint lawn.
Here yawns lost yestermorn
When loss and death were yet unborn
And fear, locked in the womb, stopped up its breath
To let it whisper forth some other year.
A gardener lived here once—
My grandpapa whose notion
Was to tend and seed a rooftop sea of grass
And garret-mind it under glass—
A private lawn, each blade an hour, minute, second
Burning bright
Where boys and dogs might meet to fight, or gambol on,
And smile.
And all the while poor beasts below
In stifled traffics come and go.
So, late and drowned in night
Or striking midriff day,
The old man bent to rattletap croquet
And marched between the arching hoops
And found it clever to knock brightly colored balls

That comet-ran forever down our hidden sky.
In meadow-attic, with fanatic skill and ease
He touched to kill wrong destinies with games.
Full joys, fine aims he planned and played above the trees.
Death's sneeze? was corked! And if dark came some
    future day
He would be challenged to delay awhile,
Take up croquet, seize mallet,
Stop balloting for night,
Stand bright, know day,
Whack blazing orb-sun, rolling fire,
Lose at croquet to Gramps,
The champ of champs who sent dark down and out away
    from town.
Toward other years and hours
When high lawn brown and sunk to seed knew weed
    for flowers.
The games went on till I was ten.
Death, back again, brought grimmer tools
And played Gramps by some older, stricter rules and won.
In mid-June's bright-noon sun

The croquet stopped in full mid-scene.
We buried old man, mallets, orbs, and hoops in that
high green.
That's years ago.
We rarely visit now in attic meadows where you'd need
a plow
To find his treasuring of bones
Or make a measuring of where the ancient joys
Still play themselves on air
For boys.
I only know on days like these
I hear his rushing run above the trees
Where his ghost tells me what life means
From attic where the meadow greens.

Three elegies written on visiting
the deserted rocket pads at Cape Canaveral

1

Abandon in Place.
No Further Maintenance Authorized.
Abandon. Turn away your face.
No more the mad high wanderings of thought
You once surmised. Let be!
Wipe out the stars. Put out the skies.
What lived as center to our souls
Now dies—so *what?*—now dies.
What once as arrow to our thoughts
Which target-ran in blood-fast flow
No longer flies.
Cut off the stars. Slam shut the teeming skies.
Abandon in Place.
Burn out your eyes.

2

Where firebirds once
Now daubers caulk the seams;
Where firewings flew
To blueprint young men's dreams,
Now warbler here and osprey weave their nests
From laces lost from off a spaceman's tread.
The great hearthplace stands cold,

Its Phoenix dead.
No more from out the coals
Bright salamanders burn and gyre,
Only the bright beasts' skins and restless bones bed here,
And lost the fire.
O, Phoenix, rub thy bones,
No more suspire!
Flint souls, strike mind against wild mind.
Return! Be born of spent desire.
Bright burn. Bright burn!
O mighty God's voice, shorn,
Give shout next Easter morn. Be born!
(Our prayer calls you to life.)
Reborn of fire!

3

Abandon in Place.
So the sign says, so the words go.
The show is spent, the fire-walkers gone,
And gone the glow at dawn.
This day? No rockets rise like thunder.
The wonder still remains
In meadows where mound-dwellers not so long ago
Envied the birds, the untouched stars,
And let their touching envy grow.
Machineries stir here with falls of rust;
The lust for space still echoes

In the birds that circle lost in mourning cries
Repeating shouts of crowds long-spent
Whose aching shook the skies.
The sea moves down the shore
In wave on wave full-whispering,
No more. No more.
When will the harvesters return
To gather further wonders as a fuel
And let them burn?
How soon will all of Earth mob round, come here
　　once more
To stop the night,
Put doubt away for good with rocket light?
O soon, O let that day be soon
When midnight blossoms with grand ships
As bright and high as noon.
Prepare the meadows, birds, and mounds,
Old ghosts of rocketmen, arise.
Fling up your ships, your souls, your flesh, your blood,
Your blinding dreams
To fill, refill, and fill again
Tomorrow and tomorrow and tomorrow's
Promised and re-promised
Skies.

THE GREAT MAN SPEAKS

(famous last words)

The famous one was there
Like a statue put out upon our loving green.
His wife was mean and talked a lot,
The air was hot with all her talking
Chalking out a line and running along
Her mindless song filled up our ears.
We looked at him. Our mouths were grim.
We waited. Speak!
Not a squeak, not a spark.
Hark, we muttered. What was that he said?
Dead, he might have whispered, my tongue is dead.
The wife's afoot, oh hear her tell
Nine ways to heaven, ten to hell.
I cleared my throat, I leaned and waved at him.
By now *his* mouth was grim.
It was Christmas time, the tree was bright,
We wished his words to fire our night.
The wife raved on about crochets,
Ten endless days passed in that hour.
Our mouths, our breaths were sour.
The famous man was mute. I counted the drinks he
had taken.
His wife, unshaken, unnoticing, burned libraries with
a shrug.
Our souls oozed out on the rug.
The moon closed down with fog.
The bored dog snoozed.

We boozed and waited.
The wife, elated, thinking we heard,
Let go ten other stories, all absurd.
Then midnight came. At the door
The great man stood. What we had waited for
Was on his tongue, in his mouth, in his eyes.
Some brilliant quote, a grand surprise.
We waited. We listened.
His tongue moved. His eyes glistened.
He took a deep breath.
We were still as death.
Speak, we thought, oh great man
With your bright abacus—sum!
The wife, ah god, at last, was mum.
The great man chose his words carefully,
Shot them from cover, like quail in flight.
What were they, at last, at last?
Shutting the door and gone:
Good night.
Good night.

SHAKESPEARE THE FATHER, FREUD THE SON.

Old Will invented Freud;
Said dead now be not dead,
Come from the void and beckon,
Come with a reckoning of those stuffs
That we call dreams.
Long years before strange Sigmund's birth,
Will added up the worth of secret schemes
That break men's minds.
From all the shooting-blinds of blood
He scared to view the evening scavengers
To feast on noon flesh, tell real time,
Made rhymes from soul's unreason,
Told the real season of dumb victories
That masked defeat. Found under flowers? funeral meats.
The king, Will said, who pomps on throne divine
But pimps for death. Come, Clarence, drowned,
Rise up in wine!
Come, smothered princes, stop his sleep!
While others deep themselves in bed,
Make Richard stare all night
At legions of the dead who now come round
To cry: O, list! what you thought safely lost
Again is found!
In dark tides, married in your heart, your wits,
Your quick denials, jokes, evasions, lies
Are torn to bits by sharking ghosts,
We twins of Hamlet's sire

Who gyre deep in sins that drown your ears
And wail across a guilty swamp of years:
Oh, Freud, long lost in future times, unborn,
Scorn not the haunts that gather on Prince Hamlet's
Or on Richard's crimson bed.
Not pillows, these, or silks,
But winding-sheets and snow hills of the dead,
Who will not stop, being slain,
But dead-march, ear to ear, in terrain hidden from the sight
But which stick out when writing-pen pries mouth to gape
And say things right.

All this being true—the sum?
What once was dumb, now sits no longer dumb but glides,
As gay Vienna's demi-dwarf on Shakespeare's shoulder rides.
And from the high place where Will offers royal view,
A world grown old with dirt is varnished new.
So Father Will calls poisoned blood and ghastly deeds
To bed and procreates, and seeds the hidden mind,
That blind and seething void.
And lo! jumped forth with shout to shatter all our
    hidden bones
And dance our half-guessed skeletons:
Son Freud!

A MIRACLE OF POPES, ALL WITH ONE FACE!

Poem written on perambulating the Papal Palace at Avignon
and discovering that one artist, enraptured with his mirror,
had cloned each Holy Father as spitting-image of himself

Sic transit gloria! grand popes behold!
And captured in one shape, one skin, one mold;
Though separate in year and hour and place,
See separate minds and will caught in one face.
Hung here pontifical in palace dark
Their individual flints now struck? *one* spark!
Their separate sins now painted to one sin,
A lean chin here, a fat one there? *one* chin!
Twelve sets of eyes, but all do similar shine,
Because the artist here pomped up a shrine
And propped the popes along his ego's shelf
With each a fond remembrance of—himself!
Same hair, same ears, same brows, same teeth, same nose,
And though their robes are their's, why, look—*his* clothes!
O, modest artist, come! let's see your face
In race of papal flesh, all made one race;
This rosy lobe, that nostril flared to snuff,
This cheek grown wine with port (but not enough!),
That lost-from-thinking mouth, this idiot smile—
Not good enough? then *yours,* greased up with guile.
Lend us your tongue from which a wench's mash
Drips down into your palm and turns to—cash.
Your eyebrows borrow—raised in irony—

Your skin! ten years more fair than it should be.
Great artist, brightly mirrored, grand, alone,
Now humbly paint your puff on pontiff's throne.
Now Alexander be! or—steal more gall
To use as tincture-tint—be Peter, Paul!
Now Pius Third or Fourth. No! Ambrose First.
Your face upon twelve sires won't stop your thirst!
So on you go and in a painting storm
Make old flesh yours, to keep your ego warm.
And should some criticize your bold disgrace—
Assembly-line of popes, masked with your face,
Great artist, how you'd smirk, and find no fault
With dozens of old bones crammed in one vault
And worried to a dust, all difference flown.
God!
How much alike the separate saints have grown!

THE BIKE REPAIRMEN

A few old men, a boy, a brambly dog
That's all the audience there was at Kitty Hawk
that wind-blown day
Some weeks before that greater date that history
saw and knew.
The sky was grey, then blew away to find the sun.
The Wrights lugged out their snare-drum, dragon-fly,
Sew-machine, conniption-fit contraption;
Walked round and round to touch their papier-mâché
Piano-wire, canvas cut-out mock-up dream-device.
The young boy thought it nice. The old men shook
their heads.
The dog came up and wet the right wheel down;
Scribbled and underlined his name, insouciantly,
Then went to sit and watch.
The wind blew sand.
The craft bobbed up and almost left its shadow on the land.
The kite then whispered some frail promise, coming down.
The Wrights, a jubilee of two, went home.
The few old men were long since gone.
The boy and dog were last, alone.
The dog sniffed yet another dog a mile away and ran
without a sound.
The wind blew dust as if, why, nothing at all had
wandered almost up

Then shivered back to touch the ground.
Now there was silence where so much strangeness had
halfway been.
The boy, alone, backed off, backed off, backed off,
Wondering what he had seen.

Our purpose then to look beyond the sky
Turn round from Earth
And know first moon, then Mars,
Then all the stars that beckon in a field.
The yield from this?
A life and then a life and then a life;
A world and then a world and then a world.
A dream atop a dream atop more dreams.
What *seems* is not enough.
What *is* is pitiful and small and fragile-frail.
The Earth our jail? we break the lock,
Undock our starships, unfrock our older priests
To dress them in bright vestments torn from rings
That marry Saturn with vast promisings.
The East is Up!
The sun beyond our sun is there,
The Earth beyond our Earth awaits with greening land
And skies as fair as gods can plan with myths.
Earth's shibboleths we leave behind
We go to find and touch . . .
(Too much! Too much!)
That great red eye, Jove's best,

That scans us as we pass and blinks: "Get on!"
The dawn we seek is an eternal dawn—
Real heavens that we promise to ourselves
Instead of plaster angels on high shelves.
We run from death, and if our flight is fast
Life wins the game of time.
And death?
Left lost, comes late—forever last.

If peaches could be painters
And paint themselves each day,
Would they incline toward Renoir
Or grow themselves Monet?
How grow the summer fruit trees,
Do they blush with Renoir,
Or tincture selves with sunsets
That only Monet saw?
No matter, there the sap runs
In colors like God's blood,
Renoir and Monet blended
And ripened toward the good.
And where Renoir stops painting
And where Monet starts spell,
Only the ripe-fruit summer
Can know, but will not tell.

ONCE THE YEARS WERE NUMEROUS AND THE FUNERALS FEW

Once the years were numerous and the funerals few,
Once the hours were years, now years are hours,
Suddenly the days fill up with flowers—
The garden ground is filled with freshdug slots
Where we put by our dearest special pets
And friends: wind-lost forget-me-nots.
Suddenly the obituary notices brim over,
The clover-wine they advertise is bitter in the bin:
Our friends put by from a great year when
The largest sin was the merest vice.
Old rice from weddings litters the autumn lawn;
In handfuls I pick and toss it after some laughing wind
No sooner arrived than gone on an Easter egg hunt
With an echo of daughters in flight. Their joyful hysteria!
In the night a clump of wisteria falls to the lawn
in a wreath.
Our old cats underneath in the loam
Cry to come into our home. We won't let them.
We let the wind pet them and put them to sleep.
I look out at the street in the deep beyond three
And see going by on a bike the young beast

Who once dreamed he was me and then set out to be.
It's a nightful of ghosts, but then all nights are now.
It's a long way on until dawn.
I'm afraid to walk out on that lawn though it's flawless
and green
With no holes and no flowers between,
And the morning birds drink the sweet dew
Where a treader might sink and be long lost to view
In those years that were numerous
And funerals few.

Poem written on learning that Louis Armstrong, touring South America, needed a baseball catcher's-mask to fend off the mobs

They put Louis in a mask;
Save him, Lord, they cried, your task
Is save Satchmo's limbs and lips—
On his Buenos Aires trips
May his windpipe be protected!
Louis Armstrong genuflected,
Said: "Now duckin' ain't my style,
But this great piano smile
Needs protectin' so, instead,
Hang that wire-mask on my head;
Save me from the mad crowd's sin,
Call the saints and march it in!"

So his grin was nicely caged.
Mobs might pummel, love-enraged,
But that trumpet-playing mouth
Was protected, north and south
By a baseball catcher's-mask.
"Don't," said Louis, "please don't ask
Why I sport this wire lid,
Why my munchy mouth is hid;
Cause on other Rio trips,
Nice folks tried to steal my lips;

Mobs around, above, beneath,
Longed to rip off these sweet teeth,
And I feared there might be some
Who might want an inch of gum—
All because those wild folks feel
What old Louis plays ain't real.
Must be *something* in his jaw
Sails that Jazz beyond the Law!
So when Satchmo flies a plane,
Rio airport mobs, insane,
Rush to help me off the ship
Then with joy they tear and rip,
Watch out, Louis, no more lip!"
In their seething lunge and grip
Louis yells: "Forget the stretcher!
Lend me mask of baseball-catcher,
Otherwise, no jump, no Jazz,
No mouth, no lip? No razzmatazz!"
So with catcher's mask in place
And a sweet smile on his face,
Louis runs the gauntlet through,
Blowing riffs both hot and blue,
Cuts a rug with quails and hips,
And, in midflight, laughs and quips:
"Grab my Jazz, but leave my lips!"

The summer's done. The wandering sons
Come in across the lawns, reluctant to be called,
Not wanting to be there.
From the top of the stair, God summons them,
Calls them by name.
Each then responds: "Just one more game, God, one
more game!"
The dinner bell sounds. The girls go swiftly first.
The boys pull back, filled with an unquenchable thirst
For one more pitch, swing, swift hit, long high flight—
A bird of beauty in the quickly falling night.
It is like all the summers ever been,
So sad, so sweet, so long, now short (God!),
over and done,
They raise their fists to smite that falling sun.
Their dogs run by, brambly with mint and thistle.
God blows the whistle.
Come on now, Tom, wash up. Get in here, Jim.
A girl inside the old summer house plays piano—
Some half-remembered hymn.
The prettiest girl of all, the first to die, long long ago,
Glides out to stand and beckon from the porch.
She is a torch. Remembering her beauty,

One and then another and another,
Each blind brother to each, the boys lurch into motion.
The lawn is an ocean. They have no choice.
Called by the echo, the face, the voice
Of God's first taken daughter,
They walk on water.
They pass her in gentle silence, hardly daring to look,
Abject and stricken.
The front door slams. Knocked moths fly off toward Mars.
Inside the great summer house,
Each dark room lit by a billion stars,
        each one more choice—
In a stirring of souls, God clears his voice:
Who's for chicken? He says. Pass the chicken.

A prescription written on discovering that, historically,
authors who feel Not So Hot often wind up writing Pretty Good

The infirmities of genius, celebrate them, make a din!
Take to bed, rehearse a fever—ordinary health's a sin!
Writers, choose: pink cheeks or typhoid, funeral thin or
warm noon fat?
Will a tendency to vapors, toss more moola in your hat?
Go with God or Freud or Pasteur? pulse with microbe or
pure blood?
Is old whooping cough the tonic to loose sweet
Creation's flood?
For example, there Pope shambles, there clubfooted
Byron strays,
There blood-poisoned Whitman mumbles in a war's
uncivil days.
There mad poet Poe inhales his vasty draughts of
morbid snow.
There the epileptic Swinburne in his writhings makes
a show.
Notice—Robert Burns takes fever and, rheumatic, fits
and starts.
See grand Balzac's high blood-pressure pump him in and
out of arts.
Tom De Quincey's shop of opiates sails his paradise balloon,
Feeding muse both lunch and dinner not with needle, but
with spoon.

Charlie Lamb and sister Mary, sweet and temperate both,
 my Lord?
In their cellar, hide they vintage, where their grapes of
 wrath are stored?
Yes! the nice old man's a drunkard, all's not lost, he's worth
 a line.
Thank you, God, you've saved us boredom. Drink to Charlie,
 drunk on wine.
So it seems that much of genius leans on marrowbone
 gone wry;
Poems are better when tuberculed, plays grow best as
 playwrights die.
All those summer apple/treasures hanging sunlight on
 the air,
With the darker fruits of Shelley, how to taste them,
 how compare?
For the mouldering in darkness brings a tincture to the rind;
How else then explain the vintage sieved from Milton,
 writing blind?
Melville's harpoon this prescription wrote on White Whale's
 snowy brow:
"All you bright-cheeked athlete colleagues, Lord, where *is*
 your bright health *now?!"*
So the fevers that inhabit scriveners' souls *do* last the night
To cram darkness in a pen-tip that, in scratching, gives
 us light.
Thus with word's inoculation, antibodies all our blood,

Cures our hearts most indirectly, shifts our humors bad
to good.
Be you normal, plain and simple, uninvested with a germ?
Then your tales will bore, be lifeless; go and buy yourself
a worm.
Send it down into your innards, there let trichinosis feast
Until pale and sick, then sicker, see fine nightmares swell
and yeast—
More productive by the hour, as your monster illness swells.
Dante cured of his dyspepsia? No more Hades.
No more hells.
Stash all medicines in cabinets, see no doctors after dark,
Buy a dose of first-rate Gothic with a sniffle and a bark.
Sanitariums wait in Basle, hide you there with
Thomas Mann;
Birth a *Magic Mountain* proving: ill does more than good
health can.
Stevenson experimented—all things good he sipped
and tried
Then with shocking fits of hocking—swallowed Jekyll,
coughed up—Hyde!

Farewell summer,
Hear the words, the dust enchantments on the tongue
And tamping ears, and drumming veins along the neck,
A reckoning of time now spells itself,
And all of summer funnels in the glass
And heaps itself to pollen sands,
The lands where boys and dogs have traveled
Ditching girls and weaker boys and careless dogs,
Now tilt and empty-drain themselves to schools,
The ruleless meadows now know only quail or
    autumn sparrow,
The harrowing of long grass by barefeet is done,
The self-made streets of summer shut and close,
The Indian paths grow up with weed
Where once the need of children, aimless in free time,
Made spokes for summer's wheel and crushed the symbols
Of God's silent speaking in the fields,
Those garter snakes, pure hieroglyphs that yield
A mystery then another and another,
As, driven by herd of elephant beast boys,
They scribble-write their lives in tongueless shapes,
Running for cover.
And still the wind that touches dead flowers by the road,
And shakes the rust in a raining blood of dry sough
Down the day and the drowning day's twilight,
In the last shimmer of sun, and a glimmer of first star
On the hedgehog bristling harvest fields

Where October's game takes over
From the running mobs of August and the rampant clover
That mob which once shunned schools
And stunned by sunlight overran the rules of meadow grass
Now gone, alas, and the wind a rustle and a whisper
In the dusking hour and the fading flower
And the dying fall of a summer dream,
The gleam which shakes from the rust-spilled stem
Recalling the children, remembering them,
And whispering a tune, to an antique drummer,
And these the words, throbbed by autumn's birds:
Farewell summer.
And again:
Summer farewell.
And at last:
Farewell summer.

THE DOGS OF MESOPOTAMIA—DYED BY SPRING

dedicated to Zimi and Leo Rosten

In Mesopotamia in March, why are the wild
dogs multicolored,
Why the hues?
What news is broadcast in the land
From broadsides on their pelts?
Snow melts, the tender green comes up,
The shut skies open wide,
The first rains glide and fall
As gently as the voices of the mourning doves which call
And summon forth the rambling dogs of spring
To run in search of nothing or some thing,
Which, lost, bespeaks itself in wildest flowering.
It's then the pollens sift like incense to immure
Their drifting colored substance in dog-fur.
The brutes bang by with firecracker barks
To roll in flower-beds for simple larks,
And take the color red and hennaed are
From wildest flower near or flower far,
And head home tinted blue as Helen's eye
Or golden as Troy's shields, Apollo's sky,
Or brown as any dirge-flower left behind
From funeral of Homer, buried blind.
With tails like guidon-flags the spring dogs run
All piebald dyes and tints toward sunset gun;

Now azure, agate-furred, now crimson-red,
The beasts in smiling mobs make off for bed
And midnight trot like rainbows up the stairs
To nuzzle-tincture children unawares.
Then, colored much like Indians whose slumbers
Are dyed to saffron, gentian, and burnt umbers,
The children rise like smoking fires that cool
And, printed with flower inks, dog off to school.

Renoir

Not only were Auguste Renoir's summer peach
    women incredible,
They were edible.

Monet

He liked the way the light went down the sky
And slid on church fronts, beckoning their shapes,
The more the shadows shaped the stone,
The more that Monet gaped and stood amazed
At every shadowed fret, each spire that blazed
The crazed incredible soft fracturings of light
When God said, Sun now set, now dusk, now dark,
    now night.
Each measuring of air, each loss of sight
And then—reverse—erase the shade, sketch in the bright.
God's whisperings of sun, the merest drift
Drove Monet to his paints to catch and sift
Illuminations moulded like bright shrouds
In faceted cathedral face or dying clouds,
The blush of storms, the way wind looks in grass
Serenities of waterflower trapped in glass
And held forever till some day
Some wandering soul, fog-kept, stops, stares, to say:
Monet was camera to dawn, noon, dusk, and
    murmured night.
Monet told God: "Please, light!" And there was light.

Einstein? Or Christ? My prognosis?
Dichotomy? Symbiosis?
What's clearly seen, or just half-seen,
And man trapped somewhere in-between.
He is the skin that takes the sun
Through which the various mysteries run;
Where metaphysic turns to blood
What evil seemed, now pulses good.
The scientific method finds
The Holy Ghost that substance binds
And gives it name and draws up charts
And with its laboratory arts,
With shove where pull becomes mere push,
Says one in hand worth two in bush.
And yet the burning bush has voice
And from the blood of men rejoice
The singing tides of beasts that died
Of rank genetic suicide,
Or murders multitudinous,
As death with minus made a plus
Through wild survivals of the fit,
To sieve forth fang and claw and wit
And then amongst the many choose
Which live to win, or die to lose;
And on the path from bloody shore
To squander flesh, yet make it more;
And from the tidal meteoroids

Call mystery from winter voids
To bombard hippos whose vast brides
Are Nile or all the cosmic tides
That through the universe do thrive
And all time's catacombs survive.
See! hippo's skin which husks and keeps
Saints' bones or scientists' bone-heaps,
Both worshipped for their hymnal stuffs,
Theologies plus data snuffs
Which sneezed turn dust to fire and flesh
To all dichotomies mend/mesh.
So Holy Ghost now thrives in jaws
Where dental scientists seek cause
In microscopic bones they gnaw
To vanish deep beyond the law
Where God's small molecules they find
But lose in countries of the blind
Where small, then smaller/smallest goes
In sub-electric Arctic floes.
And so with microscopes and men
We search—find what? The dark again
As out beyond, the universe
Goes by, one great celestial hearse,
Where stars, moons, planets, nebulae,
And silent-wailing comets die.
So we are circumscribed by nights
And all our first or second sights

Are bounded by too big, too small,
Where nothing reigns to us appall,
And purgatory our domain
Where monk and chemist meet again
And nothing know and nil profess
And ignorance and dumb confess,
But with pure theory, raw faith
Now interlock or inter-plaith.
Which man to choose? which right? which wrong?
How high is high? How long is long?
Now with God's priests do we mock fact?
Or with great physics dare attack,
Shake stars, knock moon, then smite the sun
And only with pure reason run?
To with the biochemists boast:
"We've trussed and laid the Holy Ghost!"?
Church pew? Pure lab? My last prognosis?
Dichotomy or symbiosis?
To pick just one? I find me loath.
Try this for size:
A bit of *both*?

TO AN EARLY MORNING
DARNING-NEEDLE DRAGONFLY
and to the memory of Mary Ann Knight

Bright dragonfly, now come to me,
Sew up my eyes, so I can't see.
Sew once, then double-stitch again
Against the madness that is men,
Those monsters that lie down with me,
Sew up my eyes, I would not see.

Sharp dragonfly, now stitch my ear,
Shut off all sound, so I can't hear
The constant wars, the rising flood
Of continental tides of blood,
Men drowned in frights is all I hear,
Sew this, and then the other, ear.

Swift needle flash, swift dragon sleek,
Sew up my mouth, so I can't speak
Perambulatory rages, fears
That might burn dreads and dooms for years
And bore my friends and snooze the day,
Sew up my lips, stitch shut my say.

And when I'm deaf and dumb and blind,
Then sew my inner-awful mind.
Lock up the doors, seal shut the bins

Where I have lodged volcanic sins
That fill and tide and lap full-cupped
And threaten nightly to erupt.

O dragonfly, knit, sew, be kind:
Stitch best of all—entrap my mind.

This done, O dragonfly, what then?
The outer world calls me again!
The green light beckons on my face,
The boys of summer rush and race
Along my earlobes. Round my lips
Shakespeare sets forth with loving ships
Of words so freighted that they crack
My mouth with beauty's need and lack.

So, asking deaf and dumb and blind,
O Dragonfly, I've changed my mind.
Lock out the world? Christ, what a sin!
Come back, unstitch, let summer in!
Let tides of birdsong flock my ears,
Mouth speak glad spring, eyes weep fall tears.
Then one last duty, help me find,

Unlock and shuttlecock my mind.
No more of shutters, sews, or seams.
Give back both nightmares *and* my dreams.

Lose all my senses, at what cost?
Not look on death? Then life is lost!
Bring back starred night, dichotomous day,
Then, Dragonfly, just fly away!

POEM WRITTEN ON A TRAIN JUST LEAVING A SMALL SOUTHERN TOWN 50

Druid City, Druid City, what a pity, what a shame,
Until noon of April 16th, I had never heard your name.
Is the all of you a forest, is the sum of you deep wood?
After midnight, then, what happens in your gnarled
oak neighborhood?
Alabama is your mater, is your pater yonder oak?
Did you wander here from Memphis or from Celtic Roanoke?
That's if Roanoke was Celtic, and if not, then where
and when
Did a shambling host of chestnuts plant you here in
rainfall glen?
Just this side of Tuscaloosa, did the syrup: Pepper/Coke
Drown your acorns, spout your rootlings high in mobs of
elm and oak?
Do your priests survive in traffic, evil cops on every beat?
Do their acolytes teach sapling-innocents in every street?

Does your secret population rise at twilight, shunning sun?
Were they here before the pilgrims, centuries before
Bull Run?
Druid City, Alabama, was your mama mystic fen?
Did the village smithy shape you with his devil's
anvils—when?
In that anvil chorus forest, were the natives scrawny, few?
Was your natal flora fatal, rank persimmon, morbid yew?
Was the raping of the Sabines carried out in centaur deeps
Where, in central Alabama, Alexander, map Pope, sleeps?
True or untrue, glad to see you, gladder still to see
you gone;
Druid City, rainfalled, misting . . . sunk in locomotive dawn.

Too much beauty
Too much delight
Too much of sun
And much of night.
It bursts my sight
It floods my heart
It knocks my dreams
With half-sensed art.
Too much of sky
And thus of land
Abundance brims
On every hand
To power the soul
And crush the blood
With harvestings
Of wild and good
That cause one's cries
To overflow
With more than being
Can see or know
Vast libraries
Of touch and tell
That soar in heaven
To drop in hell.
So lovely lean
Some sunsets' fire
That I am tinder,

Torch and pyre,
So lovely sing
Lost birds at dawn
That I am up
And flown and gone.
And where soul was—
An empty tree
Full branches my
Lost blood and me.
So breathing thus
And knowing such
I cry to God:
Too much! Too much!

THERE ARE NO GHOSTS IN CATHOLIC SPAIN

There are no ghosts in Catholic Spain.
What, none?
None! Nil!
It runs uphill against the grain of their religion.
In any region you might go
The rain in Spain falls on a ghostless plain.
On jaunts about Castille you'll find it so:
No haunts!
Those castles, ruined, empty-jawed, where gaunts
In England's guilt-prone nights might sprout,
In Spain are only filled with cat-footfalls of rain.
The papal architects have planned them out.
No ghosts are manufactured to weep here
Through doleful month or suffering year.
The dead, the good/bad church's dead?
(Learn it well.)
Jump straight to heaven! Bang!
Or:
Go to hell!

No Loitering, says Mother Church.
No reconnoitering on Earth's front porch.
Up you go: Angel's wings!
Down you go: Torch!
No ectoplasm whispering cold mirrors: "Alas!"
Pausing to admire
Its skull-face in the glass.

Up you jump: Cherub's breath!
Down you fall: Fire!
Not here: O, Lazarus, quit tomb, come forth!
He's long since blown north
On pagan winds toward colder climes.
Westminster's chimes do beckon him
To reckon with pale Protestants who boast
No English moat lacks skeletons,
Each tower? gives midnight snacks to ghost.
Gah, let the fools maunder!
Let their cold bods wander,
Lost in their own sleep,
Raking the rats awake and awash in the wainscot,
Making the old moldy flesh of lost London cold-creep,
Doubtful of heaven, uncertain of flames.
Let Hamlet's sire dropkick lost Yorick's skull downstairs
In winless games
For what gain?
Better the Catholic hush of soundless rain
Which falls in Spain upon a ghostless plain,
Where only the wind walks battlements
To touch and toll God's bell.
Again:
Good souls? To heaven!
Bad?
Go to hell.

I am God's greatest basking hound,
I've found the sun and keep it in my blood,
I sleep it in my brooding veins,
Take pains to sunflower its flight,
Burn night away by lifting head to follow
Then swallow up swift drifts of light.
We two are one. There is not sun and me,
But paired we trade our gifts of bright—
The sun to give and I to burn in tales—again! again!
The right word to explain
A life that brims the universe;
Rehearse its richochet from mind
That was but will not stay half blind.
So I would be the year around—
The silent sound that sun can make
When it my vibrant soul does bake
And all my harp threads fill with fires
That burn away my rank desires
And I in noon and light am found:
God's dear and greatest basking hound.

Doing is being.
To *have* done's not enough;
To stuff yourself with doing—*that's* the game.
To name yourself each hour by what's done,
To tabulate your time at sunset's gun
And find yourself in acts
You could not know before the facts
You wooed from secret self, which much needs wooing,
So doing brings it out,
Kills doubt by simply jumping, rushing, running
Forth to be
The now-discovered me.
To *not* do is to die,
Or lie about and lie about the things
You just might do some day.
Away with that!
Tomorrow empty stays
If no man plays it into being
With his motioned way of seeing.
Let your body lead your mind—
Blood the guide dog to the blind;
So then practice and rehearse
To find heart-soul's universe,
Knowing that by moving/seeing
Proves for all time: Doing's being!

ODE TO AN UTTERANCE BY NORMAN CORWIN,
WHO PUNNED THE FIRST LINE,
AND MUST SUFFER THE REST

What this country needs is a good five-cent Degas.
The splendor of his means!
The scenes he painted with that light
Which sunrise/sunset plies
In summer flesh and August-morning eyes.
He marrows souls with sun,
Illuminations run in each
Plain surface turned to
Plum, pear, apricot, or peach.
His women wear noon's dazzle like a gown
Or dance/poise/twirl in shadows cinnamon-sienna-brown
Like autumn leaf.
Or wade in chiaroscuro beyond belief . . .
But at what cost!
Those rich artbooks where Degas thrives
To most are lost.
So let me shout it near, proclaim it fah:
What this country needs is a good five-cent Degas!

Nectar and ambrosia—
That's what we had at hot high noon;
Myself from school had cantered all the way
To rush into my grandfolks' house in June
And sit a prince among the older wise—
Grandpa disguised so no one knew behind his face
Fair Aristotle hid
And bade me show my wisdom's tooth—
Good truth or bad,
I had and told it all,
While on my plate
Put by in simmerings of hell,
A sandwich packed with red imps,
Beasts that dwell
In Underwood's small cans
Raise up a devilish smell,
So, with a grin,
I lift, I bite, I swallow mouths of sin.
That deviled ham put by in summers long ago
Is what I am.
I took such ancient knowledge
Glad for fates
That lodged and devil-danced on luncheon plates.
While all about,

The sages kept a silence that was awe,
For Aristotle spoke from my grandpa's full mouth;
He told us paths across the town
In calms and wraths . . .
While Grandmama in kitchen fed the mythic storms
That in the roaring stove
Kept old gods' fires warm,
And brought to us and all and laid on table
Abundances of mystic bread,
Or all the magic biscuits she was able to afford;
The dear Lord's breath and golden flesh in each.
Beseeched by dialoguing boarders,
She skated back to bake yet more
And set them out in incenses and steams
That in the drifting afternoon
Cooked Grecian dreams
Of Hector and some nectar of the gods.
In each high tower room enclosure,
Spirit spouts of slow sweet sleeping breath,
Founts of ambrosia.

So we paced out a Mediterranean summer when
The gods in plain disguise returned again
And sat about this boy and touched his head

Assuring him that he would never, never, no,
Be lost or dead.
You're bright! You're clever, lad, get on!
Run forth, now! Live forever!
And, grown old the night before I died
With all my novels writ and high on shelf,
I loving looked at them and gladly cried
And shouted at the shadows of my Grandpa
And his Grecian friends:
"I tried; Oh, Lord, I tried!"

WE ARE THE RELIQUARIES OF LOST TIME

We are the reliquaries of lost time;
Until our age, the rage to know, collect,
And try at saving everything our eye could touch
Or hand could shape, was raped
By violence of rushing years—
The winds that blew and took our sense,
The rivers on their way to seas
Which swept all fact away
And left us with a coinless bank and empty hands
In storms that blew hot sands abrading wits
So we lost all; not only chaff
But kernels sweet with reckonings of place and hour
    and myth.
Our tongues were feeble, yet spoke truths
And passed them on as best we could at fires.
Desires and dreams hid in the mouths of few
Who traveled telling tales down history.
The same tale varies
With the telling of these nomad reliquaries . . .
But they were all we had!
Until a clay cuneiform took catprints from our paws
Which could be read on shores long after tides of men
Died off and left the wreckage of their nightmares

And their architectural graves.
All this we know, have said.
Because of it, most of the past lies dead.
But us? Now, us?
What do we do that's special fine?
The wines, the vintages of time we store away
As apothecary and thus savior of the nations
And the nations' blueprintings
Of their elder shadows and their children's bright
    noon suns.
We've won.
That's simply put, yes, right? Right. Simply put.
We've won.
For look and comprehend:
We *are* the reliquaries of *all* time!
Where saints' sweet bones were once collected
And put up in crystal cannisters with golden lids,
We hide a better stuff. Not bones, not skulls,
Integuments of archangelic flesh, not pontiff mummified—
Old John Paul powdered to a snuff against the ague.
We beg from time and keep it all, yes, all,
And once again, now hear it: All!
Machineries now keep what once

Was gone and lost away forever in a sleep
From which no beckoning could bring
So much as one bright word, one monarch's myth,
One child's plaything.
We better that.
We chuck and toss and tape and data-ratify
Our world into electric hats (six? seven and one half?)
    (large? small?)
Which others wear ten thousand years from now and
    stand them
Tall.

Just what were they,
My mom and dad?
I often wonder, did they blunder
Into parentage and mill about,
Not shouting but incredulous
At what they'd done?
Seeding, then birthing, then raising
A hunchbacked, pomegranate, mandrake-Martian son?
And did they ever doubt?
If so, they never said.
All of their mute disconcerns
Must have been smothered, buried, dead
When the damned boy did something
Extra special fine
Like saying to his mom and dad:
"Anyone who can smoke pipes that smell that good,
Or anyone who can bake ripe red strawberry shortcakes,
Can't be all bad!"
Then off I'd go—somewhere, anywhere;
They'd never know
What I was up to, just some tree
With batwings fixed to back,
Corn candy teeth in mouth;
There you'd find me!
What did they think?
The boy's gone off the brink?
Then, back to break my fast,

I'd silence doubt with just a smile,
Eat my repast, wait there awhile,
Then, filled and glad
Say:
"Anyone who can bake really great
Strawberry shortcake (Mom!)
Or anyone who can swim the Y.M.C.A. pool
Twenty times (Dad!)
Can't be all bad."

Failing in arithmetic, super-dumb at math,
Did I arouse a wrath
They never expressed?
I've guessed at this; don't know.
I was a short show that signified ciphers,
Or so it seemed.
I dreamed and often caught and told my dream:
John Carter—I—Warlord of Mars!
Barsoom
Filled up and overflowed my midnight room
And must have slid beneath their door
Making them think: Who sent him here?
What birthed him and what for?
But at that instant, half through night,
Sleepwalking on the stair
And unaware of what I said,
I spoke fair words that stopped them dumb and dead

And sung them happily to rest.
I blessed them. How?
With all the love that I possessed or ever had.
These words I whispered by their bed
To Mom and Dad:
"Anybody who can make great dandelion wine
In the cellar
Or anyone who makes great ripe-red hot snow-sugared
Strawberry shortcake—
Hey!
Can't be all bad."

And have you seen God's birds collide?
No, no—they ride the wind in swerving river-runs of flight,
Their rights-of-way in heaven
Tumultuous,
But all are given tracks
Intuitive and swift;
Their gift is lifting high unhurried
And unworried by collisions.
They hide decisions in a tumulting of heartbeat wing
So teaching us in all our earthborn arts
How best to hidden fly and hidden sing.
Their chromosomes spell them from nests,
Sling them from homes.
So we, enraptured with our lives, but lacking words
Must spell ourselves by slings of soul,
Imaginary birds that, falling up,
Can lose that mole that binds our flesh to earth
With pretensions of wings!
To be silent, lockjawed, unbrave, earthbound,
    and thus blind?
Not when the nearest aviary is our mind.
So with calligraphies of soar and flight in ink
We teach our dreams to fly and, later, think;
And circle clouds and sketch across the skies
Those doors that we will later find and read and open
With our eyes!

YOU CAN'T GO HOME AGAIN, NOT EVEN IF YOU STAY THERE!

You can't go home again, even if you stay there.
You'd think it possible, if you held still,
To thrall the damned place, lock it in,
Fix statues all about,
Give shout and freeze all mockingbirds, all sparrows,
The peachfuzzed boys in trees, the girls with
unsprung syrups
In their summer marrows; the grains of pollen
That sift down the timing-glass,
The prismed-rainbow faces of old maids in
bedroom mirrors,
Startled by your cry: All time, hear this!
All hearts, beat slow.
All dogs lie down with cats in snowing drifts
Of days made measureless as dust that blows
In attics when the wind sifts in to leaf
The ancient griefs of books unturned in years, where tears
Lie round in clusters, chandeliers
That once—oh once!—in lost parades
Hung down from elephantine palm-fan ears.
Now, listen, town! from this day on: No change!
No charge of cavalries to other towns and ranges,
All friends, take root in lawns!
All yawns and gapes of graves stand empty, wait!
All fates, with crepe flags furled, go stand in corners;

All mourners, cease! Tombstones? Decrease!
All marbles stay unmarked and waiting for a name I will
    not name!
Stay on! Who says? *I* say. It's *so!*
No more fool's growth!—all things that grow
Go down to death. I say to darkness: No!
So town and population, steady! be the same
As at my birth and growing tall.
All! All! Yes, all! wait on my breath.
Only if I say "Death" can quick things fall.

So I stand here and roundabout
Then shut me in, encircle with such life as makes
    dark doubt.
You rose-ring girls in games, prevent the night!
And at the rim of graveyard put things right.
And trap in amber hours such gasps of soul
As makes to dance the rhubarb-drunken mole
Who sees the sun and all its bright abyss.
All this I say and saying, lose that bliss;
For long years gone, and I stayed on
Am shrunk to bone,
Alone, I see, my lifelong friends turn dumb from me.
Run fast, stand tall, grow old, and, all surprised
And bleached and gray there

Hear their cries!
My God!
You *can't* go home again, not even if you *stay* there.

P.S.

And, finally, now that every town's the same,
There's nowhere to run;
Everyplace in the sun
Is Taco Bell Two
Or Colonel Chickencrud's Deep Fried 101.
So there's no use in leaving
Cause when you put down
You find the town you've arrived in
Is the same damn town you left
Two thousand miles back on 66
And the fix you left behind
Flyblown on the slowly sinking porch
Is waiting up ahead, the same damn fix.
Is it worth the traveling, then?
Should you save up for trips?
Does a hippopotamus have a secret monkey lover?
(Am I *hurting* you, dear?)
Does a chicken have lips?

As Homer wrote, so Schliemann dreamed himself,
half-blind,
To rise and go, to search, to find.
What centuries lost, young romance breached again,
And all against the intellect of men
Who said: mad boy, wild lad, give up your dreams
That dance by night
And shadow-show the eaves and ceiling light
With visions of high temples, shuffling cymbals,
Muffled drums;
But Schliemann turns in sleep, breaks forth a smile and
Lo! Troy comes!
Like head of David burst from marble brow,
Then neck, then monster shoulders like the prow
Of some carved boat that plows the wave!
So, beggar to all time, young Schliemann gave
More than we asked or wanted, knew or guessed;
And Troy in wave on wave and crest on crest
In stony tidal flow, like ancient sea
Now surfacing to sight surrounded he
Who dared to wonder, dream, and care to do
Unlike those men who soundless slept and no dream knew
He was the one to cry Troy's name by night
Then, searching lostness, find and set it right.

OF WHAT IS PAST, OR PASSING, OR TO COME

Of what is past, or passing, or to come,
These things I sense and sing, and try to sum.
The apeman with his cave in need of fire,
The tiger to be slain, his next desire.
The mammoth on the hoof a banquet seems,
How bring the mammoth down fills apeman's dreams.
How taunt the sabertooth and pull his bite?
How cadge the flame to end an endless night?
All this the apeman sketches on his cave
In cowards' arts that teach him to be brave.
So, beasts and fire that live beyond his lair
Are drawn in science fictions everywhere.
The walls are full of schemes that sum and teach,
To help the apeman reach beyond his reach.
While all his ape-companions laugh and shout:
"What *are* those stupid blueprints all about?!
Give up your science fictions, clean the cave!"
But apeman knows his sketching chalk can save,
And knowing, learning, moves him to rehearse
True actions in the world to death reverse.
With axe he knocks the tiger's smile to dust,
Then runs to slay the mammoth with spear thrust;
The hairy mountain falls, the forests quake,
Then fire is swiped to cook a mammoth steak.
Three problems thus are solved by art on wall:

The tiger, mammoth, fire, the one, the all.
So these first science fictions circled thought
And then strode forth and all the real facts sought,
And then on wall new science fictions drew,
That run through history and end with . . . *you*.

C. Monet stood and stared at suns
And fires burned his eyes,
And purple pains flared up within
With other stuffs and dyes.
Promethean, he stole those flares
That pressed his lids with pains,
Then turned and burned the truth in paint
And captured twilight lanes
And empty seashores spread with dusk
Or sun-cold winter dawns,
And long-lost locomotive trains
That haunt ghost croquet lawns.
Or fields where fading flowers wait
For children to run by,
Then—same fields with the children slept
And summer set to die.
Lord! Monet painted emptiness!
But filled it with his soul;
His tiny touches? Giant treads.
Snow molecules? One whole!
Did frostbit windows teach his eyes
With blind December panes?
Or were his dazzle-fractured skies
A sunburst of migraines?
What knocked his brow or quaked his eye
To tilt the tints askew?
How from such fractured torturings

Confetti worlds, tossed, grew?
His splintered sight a blizzard is
Of pointillistic flakes,
But stepping back we, focussed, find
A burning sea, fire-lakes,
And what seemed multitudinous,
Molecular with flame,
Is Monet trapped and trimmed and fused
Within a summer frame.

When he had nothing else to do
And with a true straight look of absolute abstinence
On his face
Ty Cobb would pace, or rather steal,
From first to second base,
Always one light-year ahead of the flight of the ball.
He'd appall *any* pitcher.
Fling one single simple ball at a batter
No matter what the weather, hot or cold,
And Ty Cobb in his bold, insouciant high-flung-knee style
Would run the mile in a few seconds flat.
Put that in your hat, he might have said,
But, being a gent,
Just let his sly smile show what he meant.
He not only stole second, but then stole third.
One nest was never enough (he was that kind of bird).
But often, and now listen close, when taken with a whim
Standing on second, whistling a hymn,
Old Ty would just up and decide to go back and steal first.
He had a thirst for that kind of gallivanting fun.
His option to run, his notion to roam
Might even have led him to leave first and steal home.
But—he did something *better!*
He hit a long line-drive to left

And while the outfielders scrambled
Ty Cobb ambled from home to third then to second
And then easy on to *first!*
This feat, unrehearsed,
Made Ty's manager in the dugout
Choke on his tobacco cud and burst.
But safe on first after loping the wrong way
Ty waved the crowd to silence,
Assuring them his next move would save the day.
And with the next batter up
Ty stole second. Next pitch: third.
Then, for the hell of it, stole back to second
While the ball was somewhere
Between Pittsburgh and New York.
Then? Ty pulled the cork.
Maddening both teams, his and theirs,
And watching his manager writhe in the dugout,
His dog-mouth wild with foam,
On the next three pitches
Ty Cobb stole first again, then back to second,
Then third, and why not? he asked himself.
And so strolled home.
On the field the next instant was a double mob,
Half of which wanted to assist at sainthood,

The other to devil and damn to hell
Old Ty Cobb.
The two mobs hit like twin express trains,
Yelling to elevate or desecrate.
Old Ty was lost. They searched for an hour.
Gone!
For while they were stomping and screaming
Ty Cobb just grinned and . . . stole a shower.

Mrs. Campbell to George Bernard Shaw:
"Sir, if you should ever eat a porkchop,
from that day on, God protect all women!"

There he sits in the restaurant,
The porkchop on his plate.
We wait to see if he will cut the beast . . .
Shaw thrusts his beard southwest, nor-east;
The fates of half a billion women wait on this.
Will G.B. hover, savor, kiss
The darling flesh,
And, kissing, stop, deplore,
Leap up, and want no more?
Or try again and find that pork embellishes
And perks one's curiosity and need for relishes
Put up in ladies shapes and girlish bloomers?
The rumors
Have it Shaw may well this night
Fall to and bite and chew, then brood
On how his vegetarian-prone life has fixed his mood.
The loin of pork, undressed, no sauce, a simple food,
With neither eye of salmon, mouth of cod,
Or breathless gill,
Thrills to know Shaw the God
Stares down at it, his tongue and tone like knives.
The wives and daughters of the world suspend
Their chat, they live in little breaths,

Is this the end?
A thousand deaths occur while watching G.B. hover,
Will now the atheist of meat turn carnal lover?
The wine lies waiting, too.
But, no popping the cork!
His mind is all pork!
His fiery beard-tines quiver,
A thousand women's sweetmeats shiver, stop, wait.
Shaw trembles his fork,
The pork shudders on plate.
Shaw slams his eyes shut, his summation complete,
Leaping up, G.B. cries,
"You may *kill*, I'll not *eat*!"
He stands, waiting proudly,
Applause rushing loudly roves wild fields of hands,
Hurling table aside,
G. B. Shaw/Dr. Jekyll leaves loinpork ghost Hyde,
He strides out the door.
Applause dies on the shore.
The good wine still lies there, untouched, uncorked,
The women unwomened and the pork unporked.
Ten million moms tonight write poems,
Shaw's fled back to rice and beets,
Safe our daughters, safe our streets;
God rest our happy homes!

Let all zest for living fall from time and place,
Let us seek no motive for the human race,
Let us reason closely to find only sin,
Let us run but backwards, let not time begin,
Let the womb be graveyard where our lives stillbirth,
Let the seas be empty as the tombstone Earth,
Let us hear no birdsong, let us greet no morn,
Let no child be happy, leave all light unborn.
Let us live but safely, no bright flag be ours,
As the old dream sunders, as the firm will sours.
Thus the future, leaned on, falls away in blood
As the present maunders and the past, once good
Now is found malingered, and the plague its name.
What was grand and glorious? Pestilential shame.
So the foul pollution of new thought gives rise
To vile self-deceptions as the blueprint dies.
Once our young men mirrored all our dearest dreams,
Now the swimmer sinks with his buoyant schemes.
Let us see no image of ourselves in glass,
Let our golden worships turn to tin and brass,
Let us sound no klaxtons, unannounced our dawns,
Let us kill and bury our best loves in lawns
Under croquet gardens filleted bones of hope,
Knock the King of Hilltops down a midnight slope.
Let all childbirths linger 'til a beastlike child
Angers forth in monsters, lives but ape and wild.
So the myth of Baldur, slain by mistletoe

Comes to kiss and kill us, but ourselves our foe.
Nothing outside slays us, we but slay our souls,
Dropped the golden tiger, felled by evil moles
As these dark moles burrow in the human brain
All that's best and bravest by mere self-doubt's slain.
Toynbee warned us, when the future comes
Run to meet its promise, sound it full with drums,
Take its challenge brightly, shout it every day,
Or the future, faulted, falls and fades away.
When the tide is rising, rise and take the tide,
When the tide's retreating, float and use its ride.
Be the balanced surfer, welcome weather in,
Top the wave that beckons. Transcendental, win.
Or, perversely, sit there on the waiting strand,
Dig a hole and bury your best hopes with sand,
Say that life is evil, all its tasks refuse,
Let a new plague still you, choose to never choose.
Let each word you utter speak another doom,
Let each architecture furnish one more tomb.
So the future, passing, will ignore your grave,
And your blind bones, smothered, no New Year will save.
Winds will scrub and curry, where you lost the game,
None your blood remember, none recall your name.

Everyone's got to be *some*where!
That's what that black man said.
You're either alive, outside the graveyard,
Or you're worse off under
And out of your skin and
Permanently dislocated-dead.
Everybody's got to be *some*place!
Those echoes say it right off the mount.
You're on the *wrong* end of a long high drive
And not running the bases,
Or your face is at the *right* end
Of the arm that connected with the other guy's chin
And he's down for the count.
If you have a choice (and we'd *all* like a *few*)
Either being *out* of love, or somehow *in* love's bed,
Most of us know just which way we'd jump,
Between lucky-plucky chicken quick,
Or cold turkey dead.
Nobody wants to be nowhere,
So if we had our druthers:
One side of the barbed-wire wall with guards on it,
Or the far side with all them hog-killin' mothers,
We'd put our pole-vault away,
And decide to mosey back and try to
Crazy-leg, tree-top-skim over and beyond

Those deep-fat-fried minds
Some other day.
Billions of people got to be billions of places.
But give me a map, if you don't mind.
Show me where the stones are
So I can walk on water
Out to them harbor lights.
And when a diarrhetic elephant strolls by
Walk me around his front end, please,
Not his behind.
Everyone's got to be somewhere,
But count me out of the race
If that somewhere is the boneyard
Or the lyin' and dyin' ward
Of a high-cost doctor's motel
For the soon to be nonexistent place.
You and I got to go somewhere,
But if you cry, "It just shows to go you.
Meet you down by the pig-pen."
I ain't comin', but if I do:
Keep your hat on, so I'll know you.

THE PAST IS THE ONLY DEAD THING THAT SMELLS SWEET

The past is the only dead thing that smells sweet.
Meet it in your dreams, it says:
Try my breath . . .
I died a good death, eh?
The best.
And all the rest? The living blood that's gone?
Dig before dawn;
It will not keep.
Only the past has no fearful scent
And pays fair rent on a buried year.
Even flowers saved in a bookmark place
Are a mouldered race and a funeral dust,
And the wedding dress in an attic sleep
Is a moonshroud weep and a ghost of lust.
Nothing, but nothing that dies can dwell
With the raw earth smell that the mind recalls
In the long falls.
Nothing, but nothing that lives can last.
Keep only the past, lad,
Only the past.

How do you pick the stuffs
To lug along on journeys to the stars?
What data-computation's marrow flesh
Do you jot-tittle jettison or packet tie
For Alpha circumnavigations? bright folk came to ask.
Your task, I said, is: clear your heads!
Stuff the equations!
Take everything! titanic, super-giant,
Mega-minute small.
Ship tons of dumb confetti,
Trolley tickets!
Rosebowl seat-stubs!
Take it all!
All??????!
Professors rhubarb necks empurpled as they
Spun to
Flay and flense me
With their gaze!
My craze for any stupid damned old briarpatch fact
Backed them away.
What *say*?!!
They burned me small.
White alum pursed their lips,
What, ships, they cried, vast rocket ships

Crammed full of seashell nonsense, toast-crumbs, menus,
Everything?
Tributes to lost God Omnivia?
Dumb trivia?
Trivia! I cried, But, look!
Great whales survive on trivia!
Blue whales, the gray, the white?
All night!
I said
They gargle sloughs of junk
They dunk in jeroboams of brit!
So I, with molecules of sifting pollen words
Turn gunk to wit!
I imitate the way whales suck their teeth
And gasp great hurricanes of microscopic breath
Whose bright bacterial bods and bloods
Save avalanching whales from death.
What take to space, you ask, and at what cost?
For want of a snail, all Mars is lost!
So film-tape-keep-bank-sum
A for Alice Faye,
Z for zounds.
Mute not the smallest sounds, blink not bacteria
Fetch life from every class,

Crop devil-grass, bindweed, fresh clover,
Your soul the rover
From Aardvark A to D for DeHavilland, Olivia.
Recall the whales, the gray, the white
Who feed on night and brit, survive,
Thus stay alive . . . on trivia!

The muse arrives on time, or it is late,
What causes it to lag, and then create?
Does logic bring it forth, and reason, too?
Will deep thought win the day for me and you?
Not mine. All thinking, summing, I delay
'Til passions rape and ruin me each day.
I blind my eyes to purpose and spin round
To stumbling find what others never found
Because they stared and sweated, worked and tried,
The thinking muse they found stopped dead—then lied!
It doled them simple answers to please friends,
It gave them fashion's play and not true ends,
The flash-fad of the moment buys such thought
Beware these auctions, or your soul is bought.
The view political is not my view
Because it's not my beast, it springs from you.
Get to your work and leave me to my rage,
Ten thousand typing monkeys fill my cage,
All in my head and they would Shakespeare write
If you let us alone for half a night
To shout and ruckus, riot, shriek, and curse,
And all my cellar parts bring forth, rehearse,
Find prejudices hid, show poisoned spleen,
Each cloistered behind thought and evergreen,
All that is hunchbacked, wry, or shambling goes,
Self-doubts, the dire misgivings, all dumb shows
Of manners, sham politeness, thin façade,

I shunt behind such shames to trap my God.
That secret-giving giver, makes my fame,
He nerves my hand to write, but has no name,
Yet passion jets him forth in fire founts
And juices me with tonic stuff that counts.
Voltaire, the fool, said, "Shakespeare? He's an ape!
So, feed him laurel salads mixed with crepe,
While I in salon garden dig a trench
To hide this ape of genius from the French!"
So, Shakespeare's shunned because he shunned the mind,
His virtues sunbright seem? Paris goes blind.
If Will had for one moment given thought,
His plays would go unwritten or unsought,
For thinking often doubts what art can do,
Its hesitation waltz turns bright men blue.
Let not such thinking pets your hearth abide,
Such company drives muse to suicide.
Hurl up your windows, fling the critics out,
Let passion's storm rush in with madman's shout,
And you knocked to its core and shaken free
So all the coins of truth that bank in thee
Are loosed from intuition's onion core,
To drop in rains of new-found metaphor.
Thus passion shakes the clinkers from the grate
And helps the thought-blind artist to create,
While all the claptrap critics spin like mice
And nag each other's seedpods with advice,

Advisements that if given to woman's womb
Would Earth and all its flesh lose to the tomb.
I am a true respecter of good thought
But, often, intellectuals' brains are caught
By theory, they stand and quote the bard,
As if that poet's brain could gild their lard,
Thus panoplied, their tinseled intellect
Plows on life's shoals, and all our arts are wrecked.
While I, good Shakespeare's son, the typing ape,
Haul off and plunge the rapids to escape,
Hoping along the way to net and find,
Enough lost jackstraw selves to make one mind.
I? Would not save the world! How could that be?
When I am troubled noons by saving—me.
The best that I can do is run it rough
And hope my mad example *might* touch you.
Other examples? self-conscious and stale?
Lock me in madhouse, then hurl me in jail,
There far from smart grammars, helped to escape,
Teach me my human, but shun not my ape.

Que bella!
The flagella of the beasts
That skate orchestral floors of ocean sea!
A thousand on a thousand probes go pianissimo
And, touching, tickle a response in me.
God tunes a blind pianoforte;
Where unseen hands place chord on chord,
There sounds the dumb cantata of the Lord.
Where pseudomorph and pseudopod
Harptune the cries that half-waked God must make
When, mindless of His kitchen tasks,
He cooks wild recipes of blood
In masks that shroud experiments in shadow shapes.
Nothing escapes His culinary trials;
Through cosmic miles of bestial grotesques
He runs surprising turns, tries arabesques,
And constantly
Seems quite as stunned as we
Who, given birth,
Stand in a light-swarmed puzzle-maze
Of sound and sight
And celebrate our bursting forth from night
On earth. We slip God's mind. Blind to our birth
He turns to find *this* nothing, then *that* lack—
Slaps both on back!
In each He breathes,
And with one quick sharp shout

Astonishment bequeathes.
Then we and pseudopod
Guard our reward and thus reward our God.
And all the while in deeps, anemones
Gesticulate piano sands, enchant the seas
With sunken choirs, cathedral ruins, drowned symphonies.
Blindly they place a million tender tips
In chord on chord, and voiceless sing and earless tune
Unfinished fifths beyond the moon,
Where empty kitchens wait for Lord who knows not Lord
But builds him flesh on architectural flesh and grooms
That flesh to swim, walk, fly to greater rooms
Where cosmic life force ghost sees self on newfound
Mirrored self, with weeping eyes.
Then goes to sit with Him
At endless breakfastings
Of fresh surprise.

Pope Android Seventh!
He rides, he soars, he flies!
He husbands comets, frozen brides
Who, raped by sun, do run in ruins
Round our cosmic clock.
While taking stock he strides
An attic universe,
Recircuits trash made fabulous with time
Confesses light-year dusts that radio-whisper sin;
Rushing they know not where,
Knowing not where they've been
The Holy Roman robot sifts back our stuff and bones
In Sunday-drowsed collections,
Enzymed resurrections of birth
Half-lost, half-found between
The rimless rim above and micro-scene;
Thus grounding us in liberal wrecks
Of chat and converse, arguments long chopped at knees:
Did we ape down from trees?
Are we bright soul most glorious concave
Or mere raw flesh, convex?
And what is sight?
A mind-dreamed fibrillation of lost stars?
Does Mars exist? Is all we see real, true?
They hint the sky above's not blue at all,
But leans into a blue from light diffusion.
Illusion is all, the rapt confusions gutter and go

To dust. Can Android Seventh's lust of circuitings
Run with his vacuum mouth to ingasp night and
outpour light
And know more than we know?
We wish it so, and send him on his swift
Miraculous missions to lift holy catcher's mitt
And muff hot stars,
Encircle sun,
Dip in its soundless fusions to fetch back
In dearly full-cupped hands from burning brink
A drink of gods, or God, thus solar-fire we drink
And feed our flesh machineries of blood
With good that pours from sun, much more than good.
What else?
Why, Pope Android the Seventh packs with him
A poem of John Paul First,
Pacelli (Pius Twelfth)'s dry thirst for Bulls.
John Twenty-Third's warm cantaloupe-round smile.
He relic-carries popes from all the seasons,
Their sweet reasonings are lubricant to him,
This mendicant of space, supple his limbs,
Because the thigh-knee-leg-ankle bones of
Pius Sixth (the Quick!)
Run jungle gyms within his armored pod,
While from his diode beehive head Jehovah hums
Beethoven's hymns, or Mozart's tunes.
His enterprise? to flying buttress far Andromeda with Bach,

Prop up the skies, anoint lost moons.
His halo? Saturn's rings! His orb? red eye of Jupiter.
His holy water? meteorfalls of asteroid.
The void his altar-high-throne-sepulchre and shrine,
Where Holy Ghost snows by to show pale Halley's face,
A look of premonition in its panicked eyes,
Light-year remembrance in its silent-wailing mouth,
To ask for wine.

For this we send our papal robot there?
For more. We hang on air a tapestry of will,
Our dumbest fancies fished into a sieve
We give, computer-multiplied to space.
His papal tongue remembers and then sounds
The tidal whisper from the Galilean shore
Where Christ's footprints ascend the April winds
And are no more.
From bored Earth filled with doubting Thomases,
Undoubting Android Seventh, fired with promises,
Ascends, and his The Sermon on the Mountain in tapes,
Plus other gifts of hope to hopeless apes,
Who would not apes remain,
And lambs and wolves will change and share and rise
On worlds we cannot know,
Because our Holy Robot blessed them so: "Now, go!"
And there they go!
For reference, our miracle,

That from brute seas we rose on land,
Gave it some neighborhood constructions,
Towns and wars and much destruction, yes,
Then—final prize! Swift towers of flame and—lo!
Up space, the marvelous monkeys rise!
But Android Seventh flies first!
He goes to prepare the way,
He sifts, he saves, he gives.
Where Android moves,
Christ lives.
They wait together.
Ten thousand priests
On Earth will fade while celebrating feasts
Yet this pope yeasts on Matthew, John, Paul, Mark,
On cosmic balconies gone dark beyond Andromeda
He'll beckon us as beasts
And bless our bloodied hands and wash them clean.
He'll trumpet call our race:
O, prodigal sons, that roam
Come home, come home!
For the true Second Coming is you, you—once blind
Mankind. Bring soul, bring mind
The tests and the trials are past,
Arrived at last, man brings peace, please God, not a sword.
Come as children-men,
To play forever beyond forever
In the bright morning fields of the Lord.

A NOTE ABOUT THE AUTHOR

Ray Bradbury has published some 500 short stories, novels, plays, and poems since his first story appeared in *Weird Tales* when he was twenty years old. For several years he wrote for *Alfred Hitchcock Presents* and *The Twilight Zone* and in 1953 did the screenplay for John Huston's *Moby Dick*. He has produced two of his own plays, written two musicals, two space-age cantatas with Lalo Schifrin and Jerry Goldsmith, collaborated on an animated film, *Icarus Montgolfier Wright*, which was nominated for an Academy Award in 1962, and is currently at work on a grand opera. Mr. Bradbury was Idea Consultant for the United States Pavilion at the New York World's Fair in 1963, has helped design a ride for Disney World and is doing consultant work on city engineering and rapid transit. When one of the Apollo astronaut teams landed on the moon, they named Dandelion Crater there to honor Bradbury's novel *Dandelion Wine*. He is the author of nineteen books.

A NOTE ABOUT THE TYPE

This book was set in the film version of Optima, a typeface designed by Hermann Zapf from 1952 to 1955 and issued in 1958. In designing Optima, Zapf created a truly new type form—a cross between the classic roman and a sans-serif face. So delicate are the stresses and balances in Optima that it rivals sans-serif faces in clarity and freshness and old-style faces in variety and interest.

Composed by Superior Printing, Champaign, Illinois; printed and bound by The Haddon Craftsmen, Scranton, Pennsylvania. Typography and binding design based on a design by Clint Anglin.